106

22.95

FROM SEA TO SHINING SEA

Americans Move West 1846-1860

TITLE LIST

FROM SEA TO SHINING SEA

Americans Move West 1846–1860

BY
SHEILA NELSON

MASON CREST PUBLISHERS
PHILADELPHIA

FROM SEA TO SHINING SEA

Mason Crest Publishers Inc.
370 Reed Road
Broomall, Pennsylvania 19008
(866) MCP-BOOK (toll free)

First printing
1 2 3 4 5 6 7 8 9 10

             Library of Congress Cataloging-in-Publication Data

Nelson, Sheila.
  From sea to shining sea : Americans move west / by Sheila Nelson.
      p. cm. — (How America became America)
  Includes bibliographical references and index.
  ISBN 1-59084-907-8 ISBN 1-59084-900-0 (series)
  1. United States—Territorial expansion—Juvenile literature. 2. United States—Historical geography—
Juvenile literature. I. Title. II. Series.
  E179.5.N45 2005
  973.5—dc22
                              2004018308

Design by Dianne Hodack.
Produced by Harding House Publishing Service, Inc.
Cover design by Dianne Hodack.
Printed in the Hashemite Kingdom of Jordan.

CONTENTS

INTRODUCTION

by Dr. Jack Rakove

Today's America is not the same geographical shape as the first American colonies—and the concept of America has evolved as well over the years.

When the thirteen original states declared their independence from Great Britain, most Americans still lived within one or two hours modern driving time from the Atlantic coast. In other words, the Continental Congress that approved the Declaration of Independence on July 4, 1776, was continental in name only. Yet American leaders like George Washington, Benjamin Franklin, and Thomas Jefferson also believed that the new nation did have a continental destiny. They expected it to stretch at least as far west as the Mississippi River, and they imagined that it could extend even further. The framers of the Federal Constitution of 1787 provided that western territories would join the Union on equal terms with the original states. In 1803, President Jefferson brought that continental vision closer to reality by purchasing the vast Louisiana Territory from France. In the 1840s, negotiations with Britain and a war with Mexico brought the United States to the Pacific Ocean.

This expansion created great opportunities, but it also brought serious costs. As Americans surged westward, they created a new economy of family farms and large plantations. But between the Ohio River and the Gulf of Mexico, expansion also brought the continued growth of plantation slavery for millions of African Americans. Political struggle over the extension of slavery west of the Mississippi was one of the major causes of the Civil War that killed hundreds of thousands of Americans in the 1860s but ended with the destruction of slavery. Creating opportunities for American farmers also meant displacing Native Americans from the lands their ancestors had occupied for centuries. The opening of the west encouraged massive immigration not only from Europe but also from Asia, as Chinese workers came to labor in the California Gold Rush and the building of the railroads.

By the end of the nineteenth century, Americans knew that their great age of territorial expansion was over. But immigration and the growth of modern industrial cities continued to change the American landscape. Now Americans moved back and forth across the continent in search of economic opportunities. African Americans left the South in massive numbers and settled in dense concentrations in the cities of the North. The United States remained a magnet for immigration, but new immigrants came increasingly from Mexico, Central America, and Asia.

Ever since the seventeenth century, expansion and migration across this vast landscape have shaped American history. These books are designed to explain how this process has worked. They tell the story of how modern America became the nation it is today.

One

MANIFEST DESTINY

In the 1830s, over fifty years after the United States had won its independence from Britain, Americans were still delighted with their young country. Politicians and journalists championed the right of the United States to push its borders west across the continent. Settlers rolled west in wagon trains, a constant stream from Missouri to the Pacific Ocean. Full of optimism about the future of their country, people eagerly sought the freedoms their land offered them.

In 1839, John O'Sullivan, a journalist from New York, summed up the feelings of many Americans, when he published an article called "The Great Nation of Futurity" in his magazine *The United States Democratic Review*. O'Sullivan wrote,

The *expansive* future is our *arena*, and for our history. We are entering on its untrodden space, with hearts *unsullied* by the past. We are the nation of human progress, and who will, what can, set limits to our onward march? *Providence* is with us, and no earthly power can. We point to the everlasting truth on the first page of our national declaration, and we proclaim to the millions of other lands, that "the gates of hell"—the powers of *aristocracy* and *monarchy*—"shall not prevail against it."

Expansive means covering a wide area or broad in scope.

An arena is a center of activity.

Unsullied means unspoiled, clean.

Providence is another word for God.

An aristocracy is a group of people who are considered superior to all others.

A monarchy is a government ruled by a king or queen.

Annexation refers to taking possession of a territory.

Ideals are ideas about what is the best or perfect way of doing something.

In 1845, another article by O'Sullivan, this one commenting on the **annexation** of Texas, accused other nations of "a spirit of hostile interference towards us, for the avowed object of thwarting our policy and hampering our power, limiting our greatness and checking the fulfillment of our manifest destiny to overspread the Continent allotted by Providence for the free development of our yearly multiplying millions."

Other journalists, politicians, and the American people took up the phrase "Manifest Destiny"—meaning an inevitable outcome decided by God—repeating it again and again to describe their feelings about the westward expansion of their country. God had given them the entire continent, Americans believed, and spreading westward was God's plan for their nation. Few people considered the rights of the Native Americans who already lived on this land.

Americans prided themselves on not being like those in Europe, ruled by kings and fighting petty wars against their neighbors. They felt that the godly principles and democratic *ideals* on which they had founded the United States gave them not only the right but also the duty to spread these ideals across the continent. Some people even believed the United States should eventually govern all of both North and South America.

The idea that America was meant to rule the continent from the Atlantic to the Pacific had been around for years before John O'Sullivan provided the label "Manifest Destiny." In March of 1844, Senator James Buchanan asserted, "Providence has given to the American people a great and glorious mission to perform, of extending the blessings of Christianity and of civil and religious

James Buchanan

Map of North America

liberty over the whole North American continent. . . . This will be a glorious spectacle to be-
hold. . . . This spirit cannot be repressed. . . . We
must fulfill our destiny."

Intense patriotism provided part of the reason people liked the idea of Manifest Destiny so
much. Added to this was the fear that America
would soon run out of room on the land it

11

already occupied. Most of the settlers traveling west liked their space. As more people moved into their area, they started feeling crowded. A common sentiment was that when you could see the smoke from your nearest neighbor's chimney, it was time to move on.

A pioneer family builds their cabin.

During this period in America's history, Texas functioned as an independent nation. Until 1836, it had been a part of Mexico. Even after it had fought for and won its independence, however, Mexico still refused to acknowl-

nation. Some Americans thought the United States should annex Texas, making it a state in the Union. After all, a large percentage of the Texas population was already American.

Whether or not to annex Texas became a dividing issue in the presidential election of 1844. At first, the two frontrunners—Henry Clay for the Whigs and Martin Van Buren for the Democrats—agreed between themselves to leave the issue alone entirely. President John Tyler tried to take advantage of this situation by running as an independent on a pro-annexation platform.

Henry Clay won the Whig nomination, but instead of Van Buren, the Democrats chose James Polk, a virtually unknown politician. Polk was strongly and outspokenly in favor of westward expansion and the annexation of Texas. He believed the United States should claim not only Texas but also the entire Oregon Territory, most of which had been claimed by the British. His campaign slogan became "54-40 or Fight," meaning the United States would have all of Oregon Territory to the 54°40' parallel even if they had to fight Britain again to get it. Fifty-four forty formed the southern border of Alaska.

Henry Clay's campaign slogan, on the other hand, was "Who is James K. Polk?"

Henry Clay

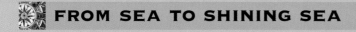

*To **neutralize** means to make something ineffective, making it unable to be a threat.*

Clay was confident he would be elected. Nobody had ever heard of Polk, so why would they vote for him? Expansionists' votes would be split between Polk and Tyler, making it unlikely either would win.

The Electoral College

When the Founding Fathers shaped our nation, they faced an important question: What was the best way to elect the President? One alternative was to have Congress choose the President. This was rejected because of concerns that it could lead to corruption or upset the balance of power. Another method considered was for the state legislature to elect the President. Many felt that this would lead to the erosion of federal authority. The last option was election through direct popular vote. The Constitutional Convention rejected direct vote because of the concern that, due to the difficulty in getting information out, people would vote only for their "favorite sons."

The Electoral College was a compromise. It would allow voters to vote for electors who would then cast their votes for the candidates. The total number of a state's electors is equal to the number of senators, two, and the number of representatives, which is based on the state's population. On the Monday following the second Wednesday in December, the electors meet in their respective state capitals to cast their ballots for President and Vice President. The ballots are sealed, and delivered to the president of the Senate. On January 6, in front of both houses of Congress, the ballots are opened and read.

Most of the time the electors cast their ballots for the candidate who received the most popular votes—but there have been exceptions. Four presidents have been elected although they did not receive the most popular votes: John Quincy Adams, Rutherford B. Hayes, Benjamin Hayes, and George W. Bush.

James Polk

who ran on an antislavery platform. This split the Whig vote.

In November 1844, James Polk defeated Henry Clay to become the eleventh President of the United States. He received 170 electoral votes, as opposed to the Whigs' 105. He won the popular vote by less than forty thousand votes, however, making it one of the closest elections in history.

Congress had blocked President Tyler's earlier attempts to negotiate a treaty annexing Texas, but with Polk's election, they felt the American people had spoken in favor of annexation. On February 28, 1845, just days before Polk took office, Congress approved the annexation treaty.

Although many Americans had caught the fervor of Manifest Destiny and westward expansion, not everyone agreed. For one thing, the West was not empty and uninhabited. Indian tribes lived across the plains and along the West Coast. Mexicans still counted Texas as their own and moved freely across its border.

Those who wanted the United States to expand needed to find a way to justify the fact that their actions would disrupt the lives of the people already living on the land. The idea of Manifest Destiny contributed to this justifica-

Then, Tyler, realizing he had no chance at all of winning, dropped out of the race. Suddenly, Clay saw that the expansionist vote would no longer be split. To *neutralize* the issue, he quickly changed his position on the annexation of Texas, joining Polk in favor of it. Clay won few votes with this maneuver and actually lost some of his supporters. His problems were further complicated by a third candidate, James Birney,

*To be **ascendant** means to be moving upward, dominant.*

***Susceptible** means easily influenced or affected by something.*

***Lamentation** is an expression of sorrow or grief.*

***Racism** is prejudice against people of a different race.*

The Sioux watch farmers settling their lands.

tion. Americans could now explain that they traveled west at God's command, not just because they felt like it.

Americans also claimed the white race brought civilization to the Indian tribes and other people they encountered. How could this be a bad thing? they asked themselves. If the Indians or the Mexicans refused to become civilized, then really the world was better off without them. Thomas Hart Benton, a Missouri Senator, spoke for this viewpoint when he said to Congress, "The White race will take the **ascendant**, elevating what is **susceptible** of improvement—wearing out what is not. The Red race has disappeared from the Atlantic coast: the tribes that resisted civilization, met extinction. This is a cause of **lamentation** with many. For my part, I cannot

Nineteenth-century Mexicans in California

murmur at what seems to be the effect of divine law."

Racism was a necessary part of Manifest Destiny. If Americans let themselves see the Indians or the Mexicans as people equal to themselves, they would have to admit that pushing them off their land to make way for white settlers was wrong. Americans saw the white race as superior to all other races and therefore responsible for bringing civilization to them, even if this meant enslaving or destroying them in the process. This same argument was often used in defense of slavery.

Not all Americans agreed with these ideas, though. New York Representative Charles Goodyear, in a congressional debate on whether or not to claim all of Oregon Territory, said, "I regretted to hear the sentiment [of Manifest Destiny] avowed in an American Congress . . . because it has ever been used to justify every act of wholesale violence and rapine that ever disgraced the history of the world."

Some disagreed with American expansion for other reasons. Northerners worried that expansion into the Southwest would also mean an expansion of slavery. This would strengthen slavery's hold in the United States both geographically and politically. The spread of slavery meant more slave states, which would result in free states becoming the minority in Congress.

President Polk, however, believed firmly in expansionism. Although some Northerners thought he wanted to annex Texas because he wanted to give slavery more room to expand, this does not seem to be true. Polk simply felt very strongly that the United States was destined to spread out across the whole continent. His views on Indians and Mexicans were very similar to most Americans of his day. He thought the Indians would prefer having their own land to live on in the West, reservations where they could continue their own cultural practices if they wanted to. In his first State of the Union Address, he said:

Our relations with the Indian tribes are of a favorable character. The policy of removing them to a country designed for their permanent residence west of the Mississippi, and without the limits of the organized States and Territories, is better appreciated by them than it was a few years ago, while education is now attended to and the habits of civilized life are gaining ground among them.

Polk, like most nineteenth-century Americans, thought moving the Indian tribes west had been the best solution. In fact, he believed that once the Indians had been educated and civilized, they would appreciate that they were better off on Western reservations than they had been among the Eastern towns and cities.

Usually, other races, such as Indians or

American Plains Indian

Mexicans, were not taken into consideration at all. When they became a hindrance, the U.S. government simply sent out troops to deal with them. When they were in the way, they were moved to make room for Americans.

To the American people, Manifest Destiny was an up-

20

lifting and noble idea. Secure in their belief that God meant them to occupy the entire continent, they swept across the plains westward toward the Pacific. When others stood in their way, as the Mexicans did in Texas, the confrontations could be violent.

Indians on a reservation in Dakota Territory

21

War with Mexico

Two
WAR WITH MEXICO

The air shimmered with heat as the sun dipped below the horizon. Atop their horses, the seventy American soldiers sweltered in their uniforms, squinting through the last rays of sunlight and keeping their rifles ready. April was rarely this hot, even in southern Texas. Ahead, Colonel Seth Thornton saw the abandoned *hacienda* the guide had told them about. The company of *dragoons* rode closer.

No one is sure exactly what happened next. What the American troops had been told was an abandoned hacienda, was in fact occupied by two thousand Mexican soldiers, under the command of Colonel Anastasio Torrejon. No one now knows who fired the first shots. Throughout the evening, the fighting raged. The Americans, outnumbered more than twenty to one, fought a desperate battle for survival. Sixteen were killed. Finally, the Mexicans took the remaining soldiers prisoner and marched them south across the border into Mexico.

The Thornton Affair, as it was later called, began on the evening of April 25, 1846, finally resolving in the early morning hours of April 26. President Polk received the news of the battle on May 9, a Saturday. On Monday, Polk called a joint session of Congress and recommended an immediate declaration of war against Mexico.

*A **hacienda** (ah-see-en-dah) is a large estate, or the main house on a large estate.*

***Dragoons** are heavily armed cavalrymen.*

23

Zachary Taylor

"American blood has been shed on American soil!" he exclaimed. Two days later, on May 13, Congress agreed and officially declared war on Mexico.

In the year before the declaration of war, relations had grown increasingly strained between the United States and Mexico. After he took office as President, Polk felt the annexation of Texas had been settled. He sent an am-bassador to Mexico to try and negotiate the purchase of New Mexico and California, as well as to solve the disputed border of Texas. (The Mexicans fixed the border at the Rio Nueces, the Americans at the more southern Rio Grande.) As part of the purchase price, the United States would agree to pay off the three million dollars of Mexican debts to American settlers. The Mexicans found the entire offer insulting. For

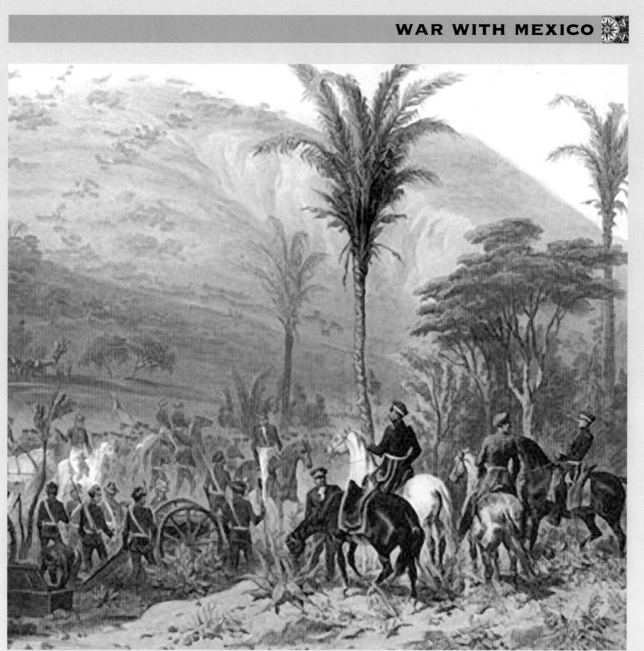

Battle of Cerro Gordo during the Mexican-American War

25

*A **diplomat** is a government representative to a foreign country.*

one thing, they had never actually given up their claims to Texas after it had declared its independence ten years earlier. On December 29, 1845, the annexation treaty went into effect, and Texas became the twenty-eighth state in the Union. Furious, the Mexican government recalled its ***diplomat*** from Washington and broke off all diplomatic relations.

The siege of Vera Cruz during the Mexican-American War

To protect American interests in Texas, President Polk sent an army, led by General Zachary Taylor, to patrol the area along the Rio Grande. Taylor's troops nicknamed him "Old Rough and Ready," because of his scruffy appearance and his solid military leadership. After he lost a company of dragoons in the battle that started the war, he and his army fought many skirmishes along the Mexican border, later moving south into northern Mexico.

Many Americans, especially Northerners, opposed the Mexican War. Some believed it was a

Henry David Thoreau

Henry David Thoreau

Essayist, poet, and philosopher, Henry David Thoreau (1817–1862) was a man who lived by his ideals. Although he was never a physically strong man (he contracted tuberculosis in 1835 and would have recurring bouts of it all through his life), he was a giant in sticking to his principles. He was a leader in the New England Transcendentalist movement, a philosophy that emphasized the relationship between human souls and nature, and the belief in the power to affect social change "in harmony with God's purposes."

Thoreau's most famous essay is known as "Civil Disobedience," which he published in 1849. The essay grew out of his 1846 one-night stay in jail for refusing to pay his taxes in protest against the Mexican War and the expansion of slavery. By civil disobedience, Thoreau meant that it was all right to violate a law if it were unjust. He lectured and wrote extensively against slavery and helped to free slaves.

His autobiography, *Walden* (1854), was written about his life living in the wood from March 1845 until September 1847. Thoreau left the town to live alone at Walden Pond, where he wrote and reflected. In 1862, Thoreau died of tuberculosis in Concord.

conspiracy by proslavery lawmakers to acquire more slave territory. Abraham Lincoln, then a congressman, spoke out against the war, claiming it was both unnecessary and unconstitutional. The writer Henry David Thoreau from Massachusetts protested the war by refusing to pay his taxes. The protest quickly landed him in jail.

The overall strategy of the Mexican War involved a concentrated drive toward Mexico City led by General Winfield Scott. While Scott pressed on from the Gulf of Mexico in the direction of Mexico City, Taylor engaged the Mexican forces in the north.

In New Mexico, Colonel Stephen Kearny marched on Santa Fe with an army of Missouri volunteers and a "Mormon Battalion" recruited from the Mormon camps in Iowa Territory. (See chapter 3 to learn more about the Mormons.) Kearny hoped to take New Mexico without a long and bloody battle. Before he reached Santa Fe, he sent Lieutenant Philip St. George Cooke and trader James Magoffin ahead to meet with Mexican General Manuel Armijo. Possibly Cooke and Magoffin bribed General Armijo, because by the time Kearny and his troops arrived in Santa Fe on August 18, 1846, the Mexican army had gone and the Americans took Santa Fe without a shot fired.

Meanwhile, American settlers in California had taken matters into their own hands. Not waiting for the U.S. army to liberate them from Mexican rule, on June 14, 1846, thirty-three men in Sonoma, California, approached the *adobe* fort where the Mexican General Mariano Vallejo lived and demanded his surrender. Vallejo calmly agreed that he preferred to be governed by the

The landing of American troops at Vera Cruz

A *conspiracy* is a secret plan among people to commit an illegal act.

Adobe is a brick building material made of earth and straw and dried naturally by the sun.

29

Kit Carson

Kit Carson

Kit Carson (1809–1868) was a trapper, scout, Indian agent, and soldier during the westward expansion of the United States. He was noted for his self-restraint, clean lifestyle, and courage. Carson left his native Missouri in 1826 for New Mexico, where he led fur-trapping expeditions that took him to California. In 1842, he became a guide for John Fremont. Fremont's reports often contained stories of Carson's exploits, making him nationally famous.

During his years as a fur trapper, Carson had lived and worked extensively among the Indians. (His first two wives were Native Americans.) The Civil War, however, brought a different relationship between Carson and the Indians. Carson organized the New Mexico volunteer infantry during the Civil War, but his greatest efforts were devoted to fighting against the Navajo.

The government wanted the Navajo to move to a distant reservation. Many of them did not want to leave their home. Carson led an economic battle against the Navajo, destroying their crops and livestock. Other Indian tribes took advantage of their once-powerful enemies. When it became clear to the Navajo that they could not win, most surrendered to Carson in 1864. He forced nearly eight thousand men, women, and children to make what became known as "The Long Walk," three hundred miles from Arizona to Fort Sumner, New Mexico. The Navajo would live there, in disease-ridden conditions, until 1868.

United States and asked to join the men. Although the men did take Vallejo prisoner, he later would go on to become a California state senator.

Elated with their easy success, the Americans made up a flag consisting of a star, a stripe, a grizzly bear (that apparently looked more like a pig than a bear), and the words "California Republic" and hoisted it over Sonoma, an event that became known as the Bear Flag Revolt. A month later, on July 11, American naval troops arrived and took over from the rebels.

When Stephen Kearny had finished setting up a *civilian* government to oversee Santa Fe, he set out for California. On his way west, he encountered Kit Carson riding east, with news about the Bear Flag Revolt and a message for American leaders that

Civilian means not relating to the military, but rather to the ordinary people.

The Battle of Monterey Storming of Independence Hill

California was already in the hands of the United States. Since the battle for California had apparently been won already, and because the trail ahead was long and difficult, Kearny dismissed most of his army and sent them back to Santa Fe. Kearny himself rode on toward San Diego, accompanied by Kit Carson and a hundred men.

As they approached California, the group began to hear rumors of Californio uprisings. The Californios were the Spanish-speaking residents of California, from Mexico and Spain. Some Californios did not like the idea of California becoming part of the United States.

Kearny and his men, exhausted from their long journey, arrived just outside San Diego, at the village of San Pasqual, on December 2, 1846. At San Pasqual, the Americans found a large army of Californios. Wearily, Kearny launched a surprise attack against the Californios, hoping to win a quick victory. Instead, the superior numbers of the enemy overwhelmed Kearny's forces. Small in number to begin with, the American forces lost twenty-one men, with another eighteen injured. The Californios, on the other hand, suffered only one death and eighteen injuries.

During the fighting, Kit Carson managed to escape the battle and rode to San Diego to summon help from the American army there. The arrival of reinforcements allowed Kearny and his remaining men to retreat from the battle and continue their march to San Diego.

Within two weeks of Kearny's arrival in San Diego, the American army was well on its way to putting down the Californio Rebellion. On January 13, 1847, the last of the Californio troops surrendered, and the California portion of the Mexican War ended officially with the signing of the Articles of Capitulation.

Back in Mexico, General Winfield Scott marched toward Mexico City. In September of 1847, American forces reached the outskirts of Mexico City, and on September 15, the city fell to the Americans. After several small skirmishes over the next month, the victory of the United States was firmly established.

Many soldiers in the Mexican War would later go on to fight in the Civil War or to take high-ranking positions in the government. For example, Robert E. Lee and Ulysses S. Grant would one day face each other on opposite sides in the Civil War, and Stonewall Jackson, William

General Taylor at the Battle of Buena Vista

Ratified *means formally approved.*

To **cede** *means to give up the rights to a territory.*

Contiguous *means adjoining or sharing a boundary.*

The occupation of Mexico's capital by the American Army

T. Sherman, and Joseph Hooker would also serve as generals. General Zachary Taylor became President of the United States in 1849, immediately after the Mexican War. General Winfield Scott, who had led the American forces into Mexico City, ran for President in 1852, but lost to Franklin Pierce. When the Civil War began, Scott served for a short time as General-in-Chief of the Union forces.

On February 2, 1848, the representatives of the United States and Mexico signed the Treaty of Guadalupe Hidalgo, officially ending the war. The American government **ratified** the treaty on March 10, and the Mexican government ratified it nine days later.

Under the Treaty of Guadalupe Hidalgo, Mexico agreed to **cede** approximately one-third of their territory to the United States in exchange for $15 million. The Mexican Cession included all of California, Nevada, and Utah, and parts of Arizona, New Mexico, Colorado, and Wyoming. The treaty also fixed the southern Texas border at the Rio Grande. The land acquired in the Mexican Cession amounted to over 500,000 square miles. In fact, when Texas's land is included with the land from the Mexican Cession, the resulting land won from the Mexican War makes up the largest single addition of land in American history, larger even than the massive Louisiana Purchase forty-five years earlier.

Even as the Mexican War was being fought, Congress continued to debate the question of the Oregon Territory. Some agreed with President Polk that compromising and drawing the boundary at the forty-ninth parallel could "never for a moment be entertained by the United States without an abandonment of their just and clear territorial rights, their own self-respect, and the national honor." Others argued that war with Britain would not be worth any territorial gains that could be achieved. Since the United States was engaged in war with Mexico at this time, most Americans did not want to start another war on a separate front.

President Polk's opinions remained unchanged on the Oregon question. He always believed firmly in the right and duty of the United States to expand its borders. On June 10, 1846, however, he sent a message to the Senate, asking their opinion on a treaty proposed by the British fixing the border at the forty-ninth parallel. Polk wrote that although his opinion on the matter had not changed, he would accept whatever decision the Senate made. After some debate, the Senate voted to accept the treaty. On June 15, Secretary of State James Buchanan and British representative Richard Pakenham signed the Oregon Treaty, finally resolving the uneasy state that had existed in the Oregon Territory.

On December 30, 1853, a final land purchase gave the *contiguous* United States the shape it

Santa Anna

Franklin Pierce

time he dreamed of building a long continental railroad across the South to the Pacific Coast. Northern states held most of the commercial advantages in the nineteenth century, and Gadsden thought a continental railroad through southern territory would increase the commercial status of the South. When Gadsden examined the possibility more closely, his engineers told him the best route for a railroad would run across Mexican land, just south of the U.S. border.

President Franklin Pierce, convinced by his Secretary of War Jefferson Davis, agreed with Gadsden that a southern railway would be a good idea. Pierce appointed Gadsden minister to Mexico and authorized him to purchase the needed land.

Mexican President Santa Anna thought the proposed deal sounded interesting. Mexico needed the money Gadsden was offering. In December of 1853, Santa Anna agreed to sell the land to the United States for $10 million.

Many Americans thought the Gadsden Purchase was an excuse to pay Mexico more money, since the Mexican Cession had been almost insultingly cheap. The land from the Mexican Cession had cost the United States ap-

has today. After some negotiation, Mexican President Antonio López de Santa Anna agreed with the U.S. Minister to Mexico, James Gadsden, to sell thirty thousand miles of Mexican land to the United States for $10 million.

Gadsden had long been interested in railroads. In 1839, he became the president of the South Carolina Railroad Company. For a long

Deposed *means removed from office.*

Exile *is banishment from someone's home country.*

proximately 8.5 cents an acre. The land from the Gadsden Purchase, on the other hand, cost 33 cents an acre.

For their part, the Mexican people were not happy with Santa Anna for selling more of their land to the United States. Mexicans believed Santa Anna had betrayed them, and when he wasted the $10 million payment on his own luxurious lifestyle, they were furious. The dictator had not been popular since the Mexican War, and since then he had declared himself dictator for life with the title Most Serene Highness and spent huge amounts of government money on himself. Fed up, the Mexican people **deposed** Santa Anna and sent him into **exile**.

After the Gadsden Purchase, the United States stopped expanding its borders into the countries around it. Within thirty years, the final pieces of America, the outlying states of Alaska and Hawaii, were added to the county. Although Americans would consider building an empire outside North America's coasts, for the most part, American settlers focused on populating the wilds of the American West.

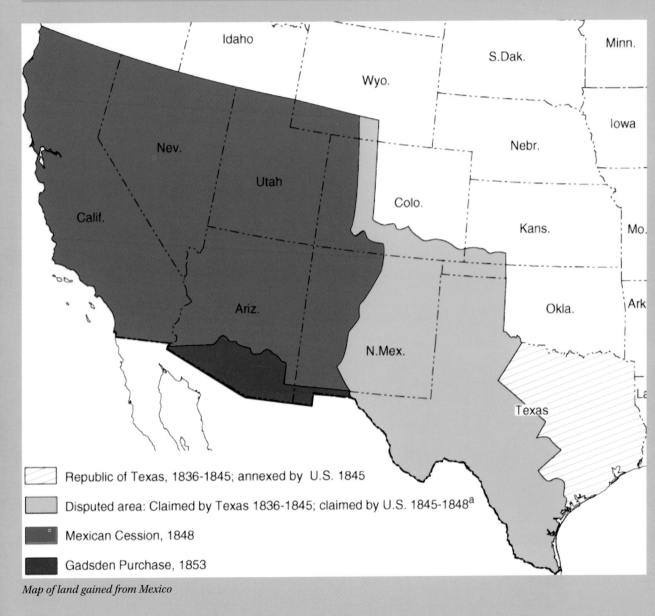

Map of land gained from Mexico

Republic of Texas, 1836-1845; annexed by U.S. 1845

Disputed area: Claimed by Texas 1836-1845; claimed by U.S. 1845-1848[a]

Mexican Cession, 1848

Gadsden Purchase, 1853

Covered wagon

Three
REASONS FOR THE MOVE WEST

What would make someone leave their well-established, comfortable home, to pack a few belongings into a rickety wagon and head west into wild, unsettled country? Leaving meant saying goodbye to luxuries like having merchants nearby to sell you cloth to make clothes, or food, like salt, sugar, or tea, you could not grow on a farm. Leaving meant family and friends would no longer live near enough to visit. Traveling west, settlers faced hunger, disease, and Indian attacks. Just about one out of every ten settlers died on the trip west.

Manifest Destiny gave a nice explanation of why Americans had the *right* to move west, but those who stayed behind must have thought the idea was better in theory than in practice. Many did not want to leave their comfortable houses to face unknown dangers. To actually strike out for western lands required a better reason than Manifest Destiny.

The lure of land was a powerful motivation. Farm families often had ten or twelve children, since more children meant more help with chores. The population in the East grew quickly and soon farmers started feeling crowded. Newspapers published glowing reports about land in the West, filled with sketches of happy pioneer families.

Apart from the lure of land, some families had other reasons to set out for western territories. The Mormons were one such group. The Mormon Church had begun in western New York in 1830. While still a teenager in the 1820s, Joseph Smith, the church's founder, said he had a vision in which God told him not to join any of the existing churches. Later, he claimed to have experienced another vision, this one of an angel called Moroni. Moroni gave Smith instructions on where to find a book written on golden plates. With the help of a translating device buried with it, Smith translated the book from the "reformed Egyptian" in which it was written. Smith called the book *The Book of Mormon*, after the angel Moroni.

Joseph Smith gradually began taking more people into his confidence and telling them about the angel and the golden book. Smith gathered some devoted followers, but opposition to the Mormons, or the Church of Jesus Christ of Latter-day Saints as they called themselves, arose quickly. Some objected to Smith's teachings, which described how a Hebrew family traveled from Israel to South America in about 600 B.C. According to Smith, the Indians had descended from this Hebrew family.

Other people worried about how quickly the Mormon group grew. The Mormons were very community oriented, and some Americans saw them as a potential threat, both to mainstream Christianity and to the economic stability of the United States, since Mormons tended to do business with other Mormons before looking outside their group.

Soon after the founding of their church in New York, the Mormons began finding their property destroyed. Some were threatened with violence. In response, Joseph Smith (now known to his followers as the Prophet Joseph) moved the church to Kirtland, Ohio, in January of 1831.

The church grew in Kirtland, but again, the Mormons faced persecution. One March evening in 1832, a mob attacked Smith, beating him, then tarring and feathering him. In 1838, the persecution became too much, and Smith and his followers finally fled to Jackson County, Missouri, pursued for two hundred miles by an angry mob.

Smith claimed that Jackson County was Zion, the Promised Land where God intended the group to settle. The non-Mormon residents of the county did not like the idea that their land had been taken over by the group. The

Joseph Smith and the handwritten account of his vision

Mormons had raised their own *militia* to protect themselves, and outsiders feared the Mormons might attack and kill them. Fighting broke out, and both Mormons and non-Mormons died. On October 27, 1838, Missouri governor Lilburn Boggs issued the Extermination Order, which stated that Mormons were enemies of the state and must be exterminated or driven out of Missouri.

Faced with such animosity, the Mormons left Missouri and traveled to Illinois, where they founded the town of Nauvoo near the Mississippi River. While in Nauvoo, Joseph Smith began introducing some of his more *controversial* ideas, such as *plural marriage*, into the church. Smith married a total of twenty-seven

*A **militia** is a group of civilians who take military training and serve as an army in an emergency.*

__Controversial__ means provoking strong disagreement.

__Plural marriage__ refers to having more than one husband or wife at a time.

women, some of whom were married to other men. Emma Smith, Joseph's first wife, did not know about the practice until her husband had already taken two additional wives. Throughout her lifetime she remained strongly opposed to "the principle," as plural marriage was called.

An artist's rendering of Joseph Smith's claimed vision

45

The Mormons still had not left persecution behind. Rumors of plural marriage outraged some, while others were more worried about the power Joseph Smith wielded over his ever-increasing church. In June 1844, Smith and several of his companions were arrested, and on June 27, an angry mob assassinated them.

After Joseph Smith's death, Brigham Young took over the leadership of the church and began to lead the Mormons west once more. This time they headed for the Salt Lake Valley in Utah. As they entered the valley, Young, sick and lying in the back of a wagon, picked up his head to look at the landscape stretched out before him. "This is the place," he said. "Drive on."

The Mormon Pioneer Trail stretched from Nauvoo, Illinois, to the Salt Lake Valley, which the Mormons named Deseret. Between 1846 and 1869, more than seventy thousand Mormons traveled the thirteen thousand miles of the trail, many walking the entire way.

The Mormons were uniquely organized in their traveling. People traveled in groups, helping each other and working together to improve the trail for later pioneers. They built ferries and set up towns where travelers could spend winters. After the transcontinental railroad opened in 1869, the trail became unnecessary, and travel to Salt Lake City became much easier and quicker.

Whereas the Mormons traveled West for religious reasons, to escape persecution and to establish a home of their own, others went West with less spiritual motives. Early in 1848, a man named James Marshall was building a sawmill for his employer, John Sutter, in northern California, when he noticed small glittering objects in the American River. It was gold!

Sutter, a Swiss immigrant, owned nearly fifty thousand acres of land and was working hard to build his own agricultural kingdom. The discovery of gold did not make him happy because it meant prospectors would start swarming over his land as soon as they heard about it. Marshall agreed with Sutter to keep quiet about the gold, but rumors had already started circulating among Sutter's employees, and the gold did not stay secret for long. Rumors leaked out, and finally, one of Sutter's employees confirmed the news.

Sam Brannan, who owned a store at Sutter's Fort—the small community established by John Sutter—found out about the gold and decided he could easily profit from it. Quietly, Brannan bought pick axes, pans, and shovels, everything

James Marshall discovering gold

Sutter's Mill and the surrounding hills

he could find in northern California. Then he gathered a small bottle of gold dust and went to San Francisco—then called Yerba Buena—eighty-five miles away.

"Gold! Gold on the American River!" Brannan yelled, waving the bottle of gold dust. Heads turned; people stopped and stared. Soon, San Francisco was in an uproar. Brannan had been clever. Since he had bought up all the prospecting equipment before his wild run through San Francisco, anyone who wanted to go looking for gold needed to buy equipment from him. Suddenly, a pan that had cost 15 cents a few days before now sold for up to $8 from Brannan. In only a few weeks, Brannan made thirty-six thousand dollars.

Gold fever started slowly, spreading east across the country. People in the eastern part of the country heard rumors of rivers running with free gold for the taking, but most were skeptical. Few left their homes and set off for the other side of the continent on the strength of these early rumors. Evidence came in December of that year in President Polk's State of the Union Address, of all places. Several minutes into the speech came the words that would transform the nation: "The accounts of the abundance of gold in that territory are of such extraordinary character as would scarcely command belief were they not corroborated by authentic re-ports of officers in the public service. . . . The explorations already made warrant the belief that the supply is very large and that gold is found at various places in an extensive district of country."

For Polk's listeners, these words were electrifying. The President had confirmed the rumors they had been hearing! For thousands, this was all the verification they needed. They streamed across the

48

Gold prospectors

country toward California. Men left their wives and children behind, hoping to find quick money and then return home wealthy. A few men brought their families, but most mining towns consisted overwhelmingly of men, with only a few women and children.

Many died along the trails as they

49

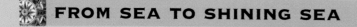
Entrepreneurs are people who assume the costs and risks of establishing a business.

Prospectors are people who explore an area looking for gold, oil, or other mineral deposits.

Prospectors

raced toward hoped-for riches. Disease, starvation, and weather all took their toll. Flood-swollen creeks tore apart wagons, pack animals dropped dead from exhaustion, people collapsed crossing deserts. For some, the journey was too much and they turned back. For them, even the promise of fabulous wealth did not make up for the brutality of the trip.

In California, the white population leaped from 13,000 in 1848 to 300,000 by 1854. People poured into the area around Sutter's Fort and then overran all the rivers and streams in the area. Suddenly, whole California towns were deserted when their entire populations left for the gold fields. Sailors and soldiers deserted their posts to look for gold. A monthly six-dollar paycheck looked horribly inadequate when gold offered the possibility of more than a hundred dollars a day. Gold fever had struck, and very few in California escaped its effects.

Prospecting for gold required hard, backbreaking labor, and for most, the possible riches never materialized. Miners, who were forced to pay inflated camp prices for food and supplies, often died penniless. Some, seeing the conditions miners worked in, changed their plans and opened up dry-goods stores, laundries, and barbershops. These *entrepreneurs* sometimes ended up wealthier than the gold-struck miners.

The gold rush had a huge impact, not only on California's population but also on its environment. *Prospectors* swarmed through the rivers and over the hills of northern California, leveling forests, filling in streams, and crumbling mountainsides. Wildlife fled in the face of the population explosion, and Indian tribes found

Price of Goods in Gold Rush Mining Camps

When they arrived in California, the miners found outrageous inflation that drained away much of the gold they managed to sift from the rivers. Those who gave up mining to sell goods and services, on the other hand, sometimes became rich beyond their wildest dreams.

Miners might make $6 to $8 a day, which would have looked like a huge amount of money to most of them before they had seen the prices in the camps. Now, they had to pay up to $8 for a metal pan that would cost only 15 cents anywhere else in the country. Potatoes sold for $1 a pound, instead of half a cent per pound back East. Butter cost $6 a pound, and a box of sardines was $16.

If a miner wanted a hot cooked meal, that would cost him $5, usually over half a day's earnings. A house servant could make $100 a month and a clothes washer $100 a week, prompting some to quit mining to work at other jobs in the camps.

themselves forced from their homes. Mercury, used to extract gold from the ore, killed thousands of miners and left toxins that will contaminate the area for thousands of years.

As Americans rushed to California to get in on the gold rush, people from around the world took notice of the uproar. Men came from China, Chile, Mexico, Ireland, Germany, France, and Turkey to find a piece of America's riches. In the camps, American miners frequently resented foreigners, especially when the gold turned out to be not as plentiful as people had hoped. In response, California passed the Foreign Miners Tax. Faced with paying a monthly tax of twenty dollars, on top of the difficulties associated with getting their gold safely out of the country without being attacked and robbed, many foreign miners gave up and went home.

The Chinese faced these hardships by forming close-knit communities called Chinatowns. A Chinatown became a small piece of homeland for the immigrants. Almost all Chinese immigrants were men who had left their wives and children at home in China—often never to see them again—and sent money home each month to their families. The white miners did not know what to think of the Chinese. California passed laws targeting the Chinese specifically. One of these, the Police Tax of 1862, taxed adults "of the Mongolian race" who worked in mines or many other businesses. Part of the reason Americans had such strong anger toward the Chinese was because of their great success in mining. When Chinese miners found an abandoned mine, they often could coax out more gold other miners had been unable to find. This only served to fuel the bitterness toward them.

Despite these prejudices, the Chinese generally qui-

52

etly accepted the inferior positions in which they were put. Since the Chinese were more willing than many others to do difficult, under-paid work, they soon became the majority in certain types of work. Chinese worked as ditch diggers, fence builders, servants, and street sweepers. They opened up hundreds of laun-dries and restaurants in towns and cities throughout California.

Before the discovery of gold, the 1848 census lists only three Chinese men living in California. By 1852, twenty thousand had arrived. On one particular day, two thousand Chinese immi-grants arrived in San Francisco to find a share of

Chinese mining camp

*A **frontier** is an unsettled area.*

America's wealth. By 1858, the gold rush in California was over; the supply had been exhausted. Those who had arrived looking for gold either went home, moved on to other work, or else drifted toward rumors cropping up of gold in Colorado. But the Chinese stayed on and made a home for themselves on the west coast of North America. Over the next century and a half, the Chinese would become first an accepted, and then a respected part of American society.

The Chinese were not the only group who found a place in the western United States. After the Civil War in the 1860s, many former black slaves faced an uncertain future. Though they were no longer tied to plantations, which meant they had the freedom to do what they pleased, few had the money to take advantage of these freedoms. They now faced the task of earning their own living and providing for their own needs. Freed slaves found life in the South after the Civil War very difficult. Sometimes they could find work doing the same jobs they had done as slaves, only now they earned minimal pay and needed to use their wages to pay for housing and food.

Some former slaves wanted to escape from the South, from their lives as slaves and the racism and prejudice they faced every day. Western territories offered many African Americans a chance to get away. Thousands moved west, either as settlers, homesteading on the prairies, or else working on the railroad or in the mines.

The army offered one opportunity seized by thousands of freed

Settlers in their new home

54

slaves. Black soldiers had fought during the Civil War, but now, on July 28, 1866, Congress approved the creation of peacetime black regiments. The Ninth and Tenth Colored Cavalry units and the Thirty-Eighth, Thirty-Ninth, Fortieth, and Forty-First Infantry units were the first of these troops.

The African American regiments served on the Western *frontier* as scouts and patrols. The Plains Indians nicknamed the troops "Buffalo Soldiers," and the name stuck, used after that to describe any all-black regiment. The Indians thought the curly hair of the black soldiers looked something like the buffalo, and they admired the strength and pride of the soldiers, which also reminded them of the buffalo. The black cavalries made up 20 percent of the U.S. cavalry on the Western plains in the late 1860s.

Some former slaves also found work as cowboys, especially in eastern Texas. Numerous ranches employed all-black crews of cowboys. One cowboy, Bose Ikard, had been brought to Texas as a slave to work on a ranch near Weatherford. When the end of the Civil War freed the slaves, Ikard stayed on, continuing to work as a cowboy. His employer, Charles

Buffalo soldiers

Goodnight, praised him, saying, "He surpassed any man I had in endurance and stamina."

Whether they arrived looking for land, gold, the freedom to practice their own religion, or an escape from the racism and prejudice of the post–Civil War South, people flowed into the western half of the United States during the nineteenth century. What they found was not always what they had gone looking for, but hundreds of thousands of settlers were able to forge new lives for themselves in the rough and wild land.

Four
THE OREGON TRAIL

In April 1846, ten-year-old Mary Munkers left Missouri with her family and set out along the Oregon Trail. Together with her parents and her seven brothers and sister—three of whom were married—Mary crossed the plains with a group of wagons and oxen.

One night along the trail, a storm blew up. The group had camped on the bank of the Platte River in Nebraska, and the people had settled into their tents for the night. In the dark, the thunder started to growl and lightning flashed. Suddenly, the storm was on them. Gales of wind lifted the tents, tearing them all from the ground. Drenching rain soaked the travelers. Fighting the wind, the men ran from wagon to wagon, chaining them together to keep them from blowing over into the river. In the morning, the Munkers family found their belongings scattered in all directions.

Mary and her family were fortunate on their journey to Oregon. No one was hurt during the storm, the worst hardship they endured. Their wagon train suffered no Indian attacks, no disease *epidemics*, no periods of starvation. Some caravans of wagons lost two-thirds of their people to *cholera*, the worst killer on the trails.

Beginning in about 1843, wagon trains started rolling west on the Oregon Trail, a two-thousand-mile trail running from

Epidemics are outbreaks of fast-spreading diseases.

Cholera is an acute and often fatal intestinal disease.

A family heading west

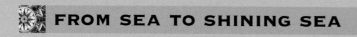

Wagon trains stocking up for the journey

58

Wagon train stopping for the night

Independence, Missouri, to Oregon City, Oregon. Settlers, usually farmers, followed in the footsteps of earlier fur trappers and missionaries.

Pioneer settlers dreamed of land for their own, free for the taking. Fueling their dreams were books and articles written by trappers, explorers, and government agents describing Oregon Territory in exaggerated, glowing phrases. The books told of animals grazing in massive herds, as far as the eye could see, wide-open spaces, and stunning scenery waiting for those who would come. Magazines published sketches of dramatic waterfalls, towering mountains, and healthy and happy pioneer families. Few wrote about the hardships of the trails.

Settlers traveling west needed an independent spirit in order to survive life on the trails. They had to be willing to work hard, willing to push themselves to exhaustion, and willing to leave their homes, their relatives, and often their cherished possessions. Traveling on the Oregon Trail from one end to the other took about five or six months. The lucky ones, who did not run into problems that slowed them down on the way, could sometimes make it in four months. If delays slowed a wagon train too much, though, pushing their journey past the six-month point, the pioneers risked running into winter weather. The longer the trip took, the more likely members of their group were to be lost to starvation or disease.

Many pioneers started out by trying to cram their wagons full of as many belongings as they could fit. From all over the East, the loaded wagons traveled to "jumping off points" to pick up the Oregon Trail.

The first and largest of these was Independence, Missouri. Throughout the winter and early spring, the population of Independence would swell with people waiting for the wagon trains to organize for the trip west. As they waited, travelers bought

Wagons had to be lightened and belongings left behind.

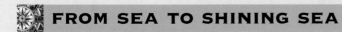

A pioneer family

A settler's home

food for the journey, as suggested by guidebooks written to describe what they would need. A family of four needed half a ton of food to last them the entire length of the trail.

Finally, late in April or early in May, the wagon trains were ready to head west. Everyone wanted to get started at once. The three-mile square camp outside of Independence was in chaos as people tangled their wagons trying to push into line. Some, who had never before driven a wagon, tipped over, crashed around, and drove wildly in the wrong directions.

As the wagon train finally started moving, and the wagons gradually moved into place, the pioneers started realizing they had packed far too much. Most people walked to spare the oxen the extra burden, but still the oxen tired quickly in the first few miles of the long trail, straining to pull the overloaded wagons. The pioneers must have struggled with the dilemma, but they had only one real option and eventually they all took it: they had to throw things out of the wagons to lighten the load. Just outside of Independence, people began searching their

Native Americans were not as dangerous to settlers as they are often portrayed.

possessions for things they wouldn't miss too much. Forced to determine what was most valuable to them, the settlers tossed out extra food, lovingly handcrafted furniture, and cast-iron stoves.

A good day on the trail meant boredom, since more miles could be covered in an uneventful day. Wagons averaged between ten and twenty miles a day, with the families walking beside them. Sometimes the travelers could find fresh meat by killing birds or buffalo, but too often, as one pioneer, Reverend Samuel Parker, wrote, "Dry bread and bacon consisted our breakfast, dinner, and supper."

Finding firewood became a problem before too long on the trail. The prairie had few trees, only miles of grass as far as the eye could see. Soon, the pioneers learned to use dried pieces of buffalo dung as fuel for campfires. Surprisingly, the dried dung burned cleanly, with an odorless smoke. When the wagons stopped to make camp for the evening, people rushed to gather baskets of "buffalo chips" for their cooking fires. No one really liked collecting the dung. Picking up baskets of buffalo chips tended to be one of the chores parents assigned their children.

Settlers feared Indian attacks while on the trail, although such attacks were actually rare. The Indians were very aware of the thousands of people moving across their land, and sometimes they turned out to silently watch the wagons roll by.

65

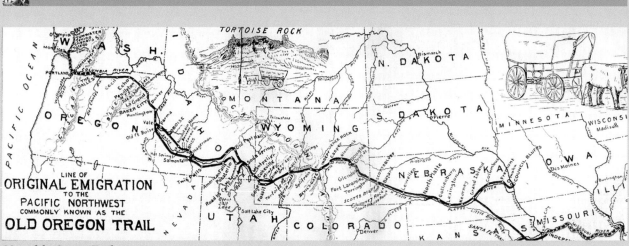

Map of the Oregon Trail

Instead of meeting hostile Indian attacks, settlers more often encountered Indians when they came into camp to trade peacefully. Indians often came to the rescue of stranded travelers, helping save people swept away during river crossings, pulling wagons out of the mud, and chasing down runaway oxen. If Indians did want to destroy a wagon train, they sometimes chased the buffalo toward the trail so the animals stampeded through the wagons. The longer wagon trains were safer from these attacks, since the buffalo would not be able to trample all the wagons.

More dangerous than Indian attacks were diseases, accidents, and exhaustion. The worst disease—and the most common—was cholera. Cholera struck wagon trains quickly and mysteriously. People who had been healthy in the morning sometimes died before night, falling ill during the day with the telltale stomach cramps, vomiting, and diarrhea. The disease spread through contaminated drinking water or food, but nobody understood what really caused it at the time. The settlers buried their dead quickly in shallow graves and moved on. Sometimes the dying were abandoned along the side of the trail, left to die alone.

Besides cholera, pioneers on the Oregon

Bad weather was one danger faced by settlers.

What Did They Do for Fun on the Oregon Trail?

Children on the Oregon Trail did not have a lot of toys, and neither did they have a lot of time to spend playing games. Little girls often carried a favorite doll with them and boys might have a few marbles. Mostly, children used their imaginations, transforming rocks and sticks into balls, horses, or whatever their game required. They even used flat pieces of dried buffalo dung as an early form of Frisbee.

In camp during the evenings, people pulled out fiddles, flutes, and banjos. For an hour or so, the pioneers played music, sang songs, and told stories. These peaceful times at the end of the days became some of the happiest memories of those who traveled the Oregon Trail.

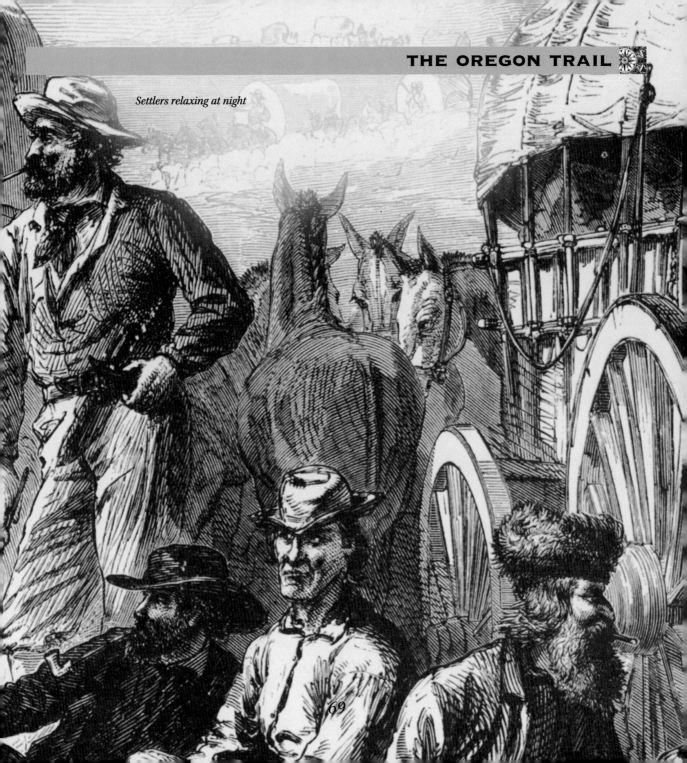

Settlers relaxing at night

69

Hunting played a major role in settlers' lives.

Trail sometimes suffered from scurvy or malaria. Scurvy, which caused bleeding gums and sore joints, resulted from not eating enough vitamin C, found in fruits and vegetables. The disease left a person weak, depressed, and overly emotional and was always fatal without additional vitamin C. Malaria spread through the bites of infected mosquitoes and caused fever and shivering. People, especially young children, sometimes died from malaria, but the settlers knew it could be treated with quinine, made from the bark of a South American tree.

The most common cause of accidental death along the Oregon Trail was gunshots. Guns sometimes went off unintentionally, killing the person holding it or someone nearby. River crossings caused a number of deaths as well. Enterprising ferrymen set up makeshift ferries at the crossings. Usually a ferry could carry one wagon at a time, along with people and animals, but ferrymen sometimes overloaded their boats. The ferries were dangerous and expensive. The cost could be up to $16 per wagon, and because they had no other way to cross the river, travelers unhappily paid. Sometimes a wagon would roll off the side of the ferry, dragging people into the water with it. During 1850, thirty-seven people drowned at the Green River crossing alone. People also died by falling under the wheels of the heavy wagons, being trampled by oxen, and being bitten by rattlesnakes.

Exhaustion caused problems for both people and animals. At the start of the journey, nobody was used to walking fifteen miles a day, every day. If the wagons were too heavily loaded, the oxen wore out quickly as well. Back East, people used large Conestoga wagons to transport heavy loads. These wagons would have meant the settlers could take more of their belongings, but on the long trails, people learned quickly that Conestoga wagons killed the oxen before they reached Oregon. Even with the smaller wagons, oxen sometimes died. To keep the wagons as light as possible, most people walked the entire route. Only sick people and little children rode inside the wagons.

For nearly thirty years, thousands of hopeful pioneers crossed the United States on the Oregon Trail. With them came their wagons, filled with everything they owned in the world. Most had very little money. They came filled with dreams of owning their own land, dreams of making a life for themselves in the wild land of the frontier.

On May 10, 1869, workers pounded the last spike into the transcontinental railroad, introducing a much faster and safer way to cross the country. The days of the Oregon Trail were at an end.

The Oregon Trail

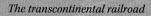

The transcontinental railroad

Five
CONFLICTS OVER WESTWARD EXPANSION

The crowd moved restlessly with excitement and anticipation. They had come to Promontory Point, a little valley in Utah, for just this moment. Reporters fought to push their way through to the front of the mass of people. Photographers set up their equipment nearby. At 2:47 in the afternoon, as crowds pressed closer still, Leland Stanford, president of the Central Pacific Railroad Company, pounded the golden spike into the railway, the last spike in an effort that took years. With the cheers of the onlookers echoing through the valley, telegraphs typed out a one-word message to all the cities of the United States: "Done!"

As the number of settlers traveling west had increased, so had the demand for a transcontinental railroad. Locomotive-powered railroads had been operating in the United States since 1829, and many small, unconnected railroads had sprung up throughout the settled regions of the country, going as far west as Omaha, Nebraska. During the 1840s, engineers began to

The completion of the transcontinental railroad at Promontory Point, Utah

Building the railroad

dream about one long railroad stretching across the continent.

Before the dream of a transcontinental railroad could take hold, the American people had to get used to the idea of having railroads at all. The first trains sped along at fifteen miles per hour. People thought this was a death-defying speed, and many were too terrified to ride the new method of transportation. Some even denounced the railroads as evil inventions of the devil.

By the 1850s, railroads had become common, and the government began looking into routes across the continent. Three possible routes received serious consideration: a northern route starting in Chicago, Illinois; a southern route starting in Memphis, Tennessee; and a middle route starting in St. Louis, Missouri. Those from Chicago reasoned that their city was closer to New York and Boston, two of the most populated and richest cities in the country. St. Louis residents felt they had a right to the starting point, since the Oregon Trail already began in Missouri. Southerners argued that a transcontinental route starting in Memphis would make use of the land acquired in the

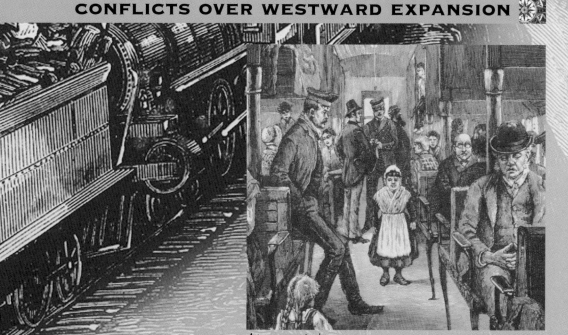

A passenger train

Mexican Cession and would bring a fresh economic boost to the South, at the time more agricultural than industrial. Opponents of the southern route worried a railroad across the South would only serve to spread slavery across the country into the West more quickly and easily.

The government considered all the options seriously, sending out scouts to examine the details of the routes. James Gadsden, a major supporter of the southern route, was allowed to purchase a small piece of Mexico that would allow for an easier route across the South. Meanwhile, Stephen Douglas of Chicago fought long and hard to secure the Chicago route for the railroad. Settlers were pouring into northern territories, he maintained, and therefore it was only logical to run the railroad closer to them. Eventually Douglas's arguments won out, and Congress agreed on a northern route beginning in Chicago.

On July 1, 1862, President Abraham Lincoln signed the Pacific Railroad Act into law.

The Central Pacific train

According to the act, the Union Pacific Railroad would begin in Chicago and work its way west, laying at least fifty miles of track a year for the first two years and twenty-five miles a year after that. In the same way, the Central Pacific Railroad would start in California and work east.

On January 8, 1863, Central Pacific broke ground in Sacramento, California, and eleven months later, Union Pacific started on their end in Omaha, Nebraska. Over the next six years, railroad laborers would perform magnificent feats of engineering as they built bridges spanning ravines, carved tunnels through rock, and wound iron tracks around mountainsides. As the Civil War raged in the East, threatening to tear the country apart, the railroad lines grew steadily longer, slowly bringing the nation closer together.

For a while, Central Pacific had trouble keeping enough workers. Building a railroad was miserable, grueling, and sometimes dangerous work. In 1865, the company advertised for five thousand workers, but not nearly enough men arrived looking for jobs. Of the men who did come, 90 percent left after only a week. Many of those who stayed complained bitterly and tried striking to get higher pay.

Finally, the chief of construction suggested the company hire Chinese immigrants. Although dubious—most of the Chinese were less than five feet tall and hardly looked able to handle railroad work—the company agreed to try a crew of fifty Chinese. To the surprise of their supervisors, the Chinese worked harder than anyone else. Even better, they rarely complained about conditions or pay. By 1869, twelve thousand Chinese men were working on the Central Pacific line. James Strobridge, who supervised the work, wrote that the Chinese laborers were "the best in the world. They learn quickly, do not fight, have no strikes that amount to anything, and are very cleanly in their habits."

Strobridge remained impressed with the Chinese workers. At Promontory, Utah, after the dignitaries had tapped the ceremonial spikes into their predrilled holes, officials whisked the special spikes away and Chinese workers replaced them with regular iron ones. A Sacramento journalist, detailing the event, wrote, "J. H. Strobridge, when the work was all over, invited the Chinese . . . to dine at his boarding car. When they entered, all the guests and officers present cheered them as the chosen representatives of the race which have greatly

The trains brought destruction to the American buffalo.

Casualty of the Wounded Knee Massacre.

helped to build the road . . . a tribute they well deserved and which evidently gave them much pleasure."

The completion of the railroad opened the West to settlers even more than the wagon trails had already done. Now a cross-continental journey could be completed in less than a week instead of nearly half a year. The cost had been cut to a tenth of what it had been. The United States had truly become a transcontinental nation.

For the settlers traveling west, the railroad meant easier access to their dreams. They wanted land, space to build their own homes and plant their own fields; they wanted the economic freedom these things would bring. The triumph of the railroad for the United States came at a price, however.

Native Americans had been pushed further and further west ever since Europeans had colonized the Atlantic coastline. With settlers gradually filling the land from coast to coast, Indians had nowhere left to go. Their ancestral lands were quickly disappearing under American cities and towns.

The Indians along the route of the transcontinental railroad watched the first trains with dismay. They did not want the white man's iron beasts roaring across their land. Worse, the railroad companies slaughtered countless buffalo to feed their hungry workers. The vast buffalo herds of the past had already dwindled, their numbers decimated by the thousands pouring into the West. The buffalo were a fundamental part of Indian life, both for food and for ceremonial reasons. Angry at the intrusion, Indian war parties attacked and killed groups of workers, destroyed train cars, and derailed engines. The railroad companies increased their security and continued building.

Whenever the U.S. government did business with the Indians, they made treaties, promising Indians the rights to certain pieces of land. Unfortunately, as settlers pushed west, these treaties were often ignored. When the government wanted a transcontinental railroad built, they wrote in the Pacific Railroad Act: "The United States shall extinguish as rapidly as may be, the Indian titles to all lands falling under the operation of this act, and required for the said right of way and grants hereinafter made." In other words, the United States needed to take Indian land to build the railroad.

Everywhere American civilization went, the lives of the Indians would never be the same. Whenever they became a nuisance, they were "dealt with." During the California gold rush, thousands were massacred to get them quickly off the land—their land—where prospectors hoped to find new veins of gold ore. By the end of the nineteenth century, most Indians lived on

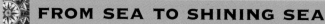

reservations, small pieces of land set aside for them by the government. No longer could they roam the hills and plains freely. The Indians had once had all that American pioneers wanted: lots of land, space, and freedom. Now, they were forced to accept American civilization, exchanging their lifestyle for the sake of the great "American dream."

The story of American expansion into the West is bittersweet. The triumph of the pioneer spirit—brave people facing the dangers of the wild and aching loneliness to achieve their dreams—is intertwined with the tragedy of the destruction of the Indian way of life. America became a great nation, stretching thousands of miles from the Atlantic Ocean to the Pacific—and as a result, Native life was changed forever.

Americans could not always reconcile the reality of their actions with the conflicting reality of their ideals. But the United States was fast becoming a powerful force. With the struggles, tragedies, and victories of the pioneer days behind them, the country moved on toward a new century.

Theodore Judah

Theodore Judah's Dream

They called him "Crazy Judah." All he talked about was the railroad. As a railroad engineer, Judah helped build railroads in Massachusetts, Vermont, and New York. Then, in 1854, Judah and his wife, Anna, traveled to California so he could run the new Sacramento Valley Railroad, the first railroad company on the West Coast. Judah did not mind working on small railroads, but he had bigger dreams. He wanted to build the first transcontinental railroad, connecting the entire country. For the next eight years, Judah surveyed routes, made sketches, and pleaded with Congress to finance his vision. His wife worked with him, the couple battling exhaustion and frustration along the way.

Finally, in 1862, Congress passed the Pacific Railroad Act authorizing the construction of the transcontinental railroad. In January 1863, Judah attended the groundbreaking ceremony for the Central Pacific Railroad in Sacramento, standing quietly out of the spotlight while the company owners turned over the first shovelfuls of earth.

By this time, Judah was physically and emotionally drained from trying to raise more money to finance the railroad construction. The owners of the railroad company disgusted him with their unethical, greedy business practices. In October 1863, while traveling to New York City with Anna to meet with more potential investors, Judah fell ill with yellow fever. He died on November 2, without seeing the fulfillment of his dream. The final spike of the transcontinental railroad was pounded home on what would have been Theodore and Anna Judah's 22nd wedding anniversary.

November 1844 James Polk is elected President under an expansionist platform.

1838 The Mormons move from Ohio to Jackson County, Missouri.

1830 Joseph Smith founds the Mormon Church in western New York State.

June 1844 The Mormons begin the move to the Salt Lake Valley in Utah.

1843 Wagon trains begin rolling west on the Oregon Trail.

January 1831 The Mormons move from New York to Kirtland, Ohio.

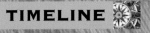
August 18, 1846 United States forces take Santa Fe, New Mexico.

1845 John O'Sullivan coins the phrase "Manifest Destiny."

May 13, 1846 The United States officially declares war on Mexico.

February 28, 1845 Congress approves the annexation of Texas.

June 14, 1846 Americans take California from the Mexicans.

June 15, 1846 The Oregon Treaty with Great Britain set the border of the Oregon Territory.

1848 James Marshall discovers gold in the American River at Sutter's Fort, California.

February 2, 1848 The Treaty of Guadalupe Hidalgo ends the Mexican-American War.

December 1848 President Polk confirms the discovery of gold, touching off the gold rush.

December 30, 1853 The United States buys 30,000 square miles of Mexican land.

January 13, 1847 The Articles of Capitulation signed, ending California part of Mexican-American War.

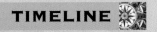

May 10, 1869 The transcontinental railroad is completed.

July 1, 1862 President Abraham Lincoln signs the Pacific Railroad Act.

1865 Central Pacific begins hiring Chinese workers to build the railroad.

January 8, 1863 The Central Pacific Railroad Company breaks ground in Sacramento, California.

July 28, 1866 Congress approves the creation of peacetime black regiments.

December 1863 The Union Pacific Railroad Company breaks ground in Omaha, Nebraska.

FURTHER READING

Bloch, Louis M., Jr., ed. *Overland to California in 1859: A Guide for Wagon Train Travelers*. Cleveland, Ohio: Bloch and Company, 1990.

Blumberg, Rhoda. *The Great American Gold Rush*. New York: Bradbury Press, 1989.

Brash, Sarah, ed. *Defiant Chiefs*. Richmond, Va.: Time-Life Books, 1997.

Brash, Sarah, ed. *Settling the West*. Richmond, Va.: Time-Life Books, 1996.

Chidsey, Donald Barr. *The War with Mexico*. New York: Crown Publishers, 1998.

Hoobler, Dorothy, and Thomas Hoobler. *The Chinese American Family Album*. New York: Oxford University Press, 1994.

Ketchum, Liza. *The Gold Rush*. Boston: Little, Brown and Company, 1996.

Macdonald, Fiona. *First Facts About the American Frontier*. New York: Peter Bedrick Books, 1996.

Murphy, Claire Rudolf, and Jane G. Haigh. *Children of the Gold Rush*. Boulder, Colo.: Roberts Rinehart, 1999.

Nardo, Don. *The Mexican-American War*. San Diego, Calif.: Lucent Books, 1999.

Nash, Carol Rust. *The Mormon Trail and the Latter-Day Saints in American History*. Springfield, N.J.: Enslow Publishers, 1999.

Reeder, Colonel Red. *The Story of the Mexican War*. New York: Meredith Press, 1997.

Sandler, Martin W. *Pioneers*. New York: HarperCollins, 1994.

Schlissel, Lillian. *Black Frontiers: A History of African American Heroes in the Old West*. New York: Aladdin Paperbacks, 2000.

Smith, Carter, ed. *The Conquest of the West*. Brookfield, Conn.: Millbrook Press, 1992.

Steedman, Scott. *A Frontier Fort on the Oregon Trail*. New York: Peter Bedrick Books, 1993.

Stovall, TaRessa. *The Buffalo Soldiers*. Philadelphia: Chelsea House, 1997.

Torr, James D., ed. *Westward Expansion*. San Diego, Calif.: Greenhaven Press, 2003.

Ward, Geoffrey C. *The West*. Boston: Little, Brown and Company, 1996.

Williams, Jean Kinney. *The Mormons*. New York: Franklin Watts, 1996.

O'Brien, Steven. *Ulysses S. Grant.* New York: Chelsea House, 1991.

Ray, Delia. *A Nation Torn: The Story of How the Civil War Began.* New York: Puffin, 1996.

Reef, Catherine. *Gettysburg.* New York: Dillon, 1992.

Shorto, Russell. *Abraham Lincoln and the End of Slavery.* Brookfield, Conn.: Millbrook, 1991.

Smith, Carter, ed. *One Nation Again.* Brookfield, Conn.: Millbrook, 1993.

Smith, Carter, ed. *Prelude to War.* Brookfield, Conn.: Millbrook, 1993.

Weidhorn, Manfred. *Robert E. Lee.* New York: Atheneum, 1988.

FOR MORE INFORMATION

Mexican-American War
www.pbs.org/kera/usmexicanwar

California Gold Rush
www.calgoldrush.com

African Americans in the West
americanhistory.si.edu/paac/aquest

Oregon Trail
www.isu.edu/~trinmich/Oregontrail

Transcontinental Railroad
www.pbs.org/wgbh/amex/tcrr

Publisher's note:
The Web sites listed on these pages were active at the time of publication. The publisher is not responsible for Web sites that have changed their addresses or discontinued operation since the date of publication. The publisher will review and update the Web sites upon each reprint.

INDEX

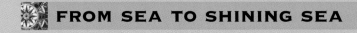 **FROM SEA TO SHINING SEA**

BIOGRAPHIES

AUTHOR

Sheila Nelson has always been fascinated with history and the lives of historical figures. She enjoys studying history and learning more about the events and people that have shaped our world. Sheila has written several books on history and other subjects. Recently, she completed a master's degree and now lives in Rochester, New York, with her husband and their baby daughter.

SERIES CONSULTANT

Dr. Jack N. Rakove is a professor of history and American studies at Stanford University, where he is director of American studies. The winner of the 1997 Pulitzer Prize in history, Dr. Rakove is the author of *The Unfinished Election of 2000, Constitutional Culture and Democratic Rule,* and *James Madison and the Creation of the American Republic.* He is also the president of the Society for the History of the Early American Republic.

PICTURE CREDITS